CW00740762

Penguin Specials fill a gap. Written by some of today's most exciting and insightful writers, they are short enough to be read in a single sitting — when you're stuck on a train; in your lunch hour; between dinner and bedtime. Specials can provide a thought-provoking opinion, a primer to bring you up to date, or a striking piece of fiction. They are concise, original and affordable.

To browse digital and print Penguin Specials titles, please refer to **www.penguin.com.au/penguinspecials**

The Siege of Tsingtao:

The only battle of the First
World War to be fought in
East Asia

JONATHAN FENBY

PENGUIN BOOKS

Published by the Penguin Group
Penguin Group (Australia)
707 Collins Street, Melbourne, Victoria 3008, Australia
(a division of Penguin Australia Pty Ltd)
Penguin Group (USA) Inc.
375 Hudson Street, New York, New York 10014, USA
Penguin Group (Canada)
90 Eglinton Avenue East, Suite 700, Toronto, Canada ON M4P 2Y3
(a division of Penguin Canada Books Inc.)
Penguin Books Ltd
80 Strand, London WC2R 0RL, England
Penguin Ireland
25 St Stephen's Green, Dublin 2, Ireland
(a division of Penguin Books Ltd)
Penguin Books India Pvt Ltd
11 Community Centre, Panchsheel Park, New Delhi – 110 017, India
Penguin Group (NZ)
67 Apollo Drive, Rosedale, North Shore 0632, New Zealand
(a division of Penguin New Zealand Pty Ltd)
Penguin Books (South Africa) (Pty) Ltd
Rosebank Office Park, Block D, 181 Jan Smuts Avenue, Parktown North,
Johannesburg 2196, South Africa
Penguin (Beijing) Ltd
7F, Tower B, Jiaming Center, 27 East Third Ring Road North, Chaoyang
District, Beijing 100020, China

Penguin Books Ltd, Registered Offices: 80 Strand, London, WC2R 0RL,
England

First published by Penguin Group (Australia) in association with Penguin
(Beijing) Ltd, 2014

Copyright © Jonathan Fenby, 2014

The moral right of the author has been asserted

penguin.com.cn

ISBN: 9780143800118

CONTENTS

A NOTE ON

CHINESE USAGE

Chinese names have generally been rendered in the Wade-Giles transliteration system current in 1914 since this is used in contemporary documents and quotations. As such Tsingtao is modern day Qingdao; Shantung is Shandong; Kiaochow is Jiaozhou etc. To confuse matters Tsingtao was sometimes rendered at the time as Tsingtau.

'The greatest prize'

Dots on the horizon appeared in the early morning haze in the late summer of 1914. Unlike similar apparitions at that time of day and in those parts, they did not go away. Rather, as the dawn broke, so did the outline of the ships become more precise.

'They're coming,' a watchman at the harbour shouted into his speaking tube. Other sentries echoed him. 'The whole horizon is swarming with ships,' one reported. There were fifteen naval vessels in all.[1]

The shore batteries elevated their guns to confront the intruders. But the ships stopped, 15 miles off shore, out of artillery range and beyond the mines laid by the defenders. Their admiral sent a wireless message asking for permission to dispatch a steam launch to inspect the harbour. Not surprisingly, the local commander refused.

The admiral radioed a second message, announcing that the port was now blockaded. His country's demand was simple – unconditional surrender. Neutrals, including holidaymakers enjoying a summer break by the sea, were given twenty-four hours to leave. The fleet's destroyers pulverised two small uninhabited islands. One of the ships strayed into range of the shore guns and attracted a single shell that fell wide. There was an engagement on the glassy sea between an attacking destroyer and a defending torpedo boat which ended when the former retreated under heavy fire with three dead and six wounded.

Thus began the only armed clash of the First World War in East Asia, which culminated in a battle on shore that saw Japanese and British troops fight for the main German military position at the settlement of Tsingtao. The defenders never had a chance, cut off from reinforcements and supplies, hit by heavy rain that washed away their positions, subjected to heavy and accurate artillery bombardment from small aircraft. 'God be with you in the difficult struggle. I think of you.' Kaiser Wilhelm had cabled the garrison which held the key to his ambitions to spread the German Empire into Asia. 'I guarantee the utmost fulfilment of duty,' the Governor replied.[2]

With some 32000 troops involved, a death toll of less than 500 and fewer than 2000 wounded, the battle of Tsingtao was a tiny affair compared to the conflict being fought in Europe. At that time, hundreds of thousands died as the German army pushed forward towards the River Marne in France and routed the Russians at the Battle of Tannenberg. But, coming at a time of retreat in Europe, it was a tonic from afar, provoking a note circulated to the British Cabinet to call the taking of Tsingtao 'the heaviest blow delivered at German world-power' and 'the greatest prize' won from Germany in the war to date.[3]

More importantly, events on the Shantung peninsula in the second half of 1914 helped to shape the twentieth century relationship between the two major regional powers and ensured that the First World War would not extend there beyond 1914, as Germany's East Asia naval squadron was deprived of an operational base and was subsequently destroyed by the British in an encounter off the Falkland Islands as it tried to return to Europe.

Following Japan's crushing defeat of the Chinese empire in 1894–95 and its more hard-fought victory over Russia in 1904–05, the naval and shore battle marked a fresh advance by the rising regional nation where militarism was boosted by this second triumph over a European adversary. Japan had declared war on Germany four days before starting the blockade, and China promptly cancelled the concession agreement it had reached with the Kaiser's Reich in Shantung sixteen years earlier.

Though 140000 Chinese labourers went to work on building trenches and other support work on the Western Front, the government in Peking did not itself declare war on Germany for another three years and it was Britain's Asian ally in the Battle of Tsingtao which reaped the reward granted at the Treaty of Versailles of having German rights in the concession transferred to it. This sparked protests in Peking that would develop into a major reformist movement calling for 'science and democracy' to modernise the most populous nation on earth, which influenced Chinese thinkers, writers and politicians including Mao Tse-tung. To protest at the transfer of the German concessions to Japan, the republican government, which had succeeded the Qing dynasty, refused to sign the Treaty of Versailles.

This helped to set Japan en route to the occupation of Manchuria, full-scale war with China from 1937 to 1945 and Pearl Harbour. The legacy of that unfolding twentieth century story remains important a hundred years after Admiral Sadakichi Kato blockaded the port of Tsingtao on August 27. The tension that flared between China and Japan over ownership of the Senkaku/Diaoyu Islands in 2012–13 showed how potent history remains. The battle on the Shantung peninsula has its place in that story which shapes the present and future of a region with 1.5 billion inhabitants and the world's second and third largest economies.

Japan on the March

The two decades before the Battle of Tsingtao had been a time of trauma for the Chinese empire as the balance of power in East Asia changed dramatically. The Qing dynasty, heirs to a tradition stretching back two millennia, had survived huge revolts in the mid-nineteenth century but then grew steadily weaker and more antiquated as it failed to adopt modern economic, political and social methods at odds with its traditions. Across the East China Sea, however, Japan modernised with a vengeance. The arrival of Commodore Perry with his powerful naval ships in the mid-1850s opened up the country. The Meiji Restoration of 1868 restored imperial rule in place of the previously dominant shogunate. Under Emperor Meiji, the nation's spiritual guide, leading figures set out to combine Western technological advances and methods with Eastern values. After 250 years of self-imposed isolation during which China had been the dominant power in East Asia, Meiji Japan now defined its strategic security in terms of concentric circles of influence radiating out from the home islands. The army was modernised and a powerful navy was constituted with state-of-the-art battleships and cruisers. The imperial state took over feudal domains, which were then leased out to farmers. Conscription was introduced. Industrialisation was pursued – coal output rose tenfold in the last quarter of the nineteenth century; the number of steamships went from 26 to nearly 800 and railway tracks from 18 miles to 4,700 miles between 1873 and 1904.

A few Chinese entrepreneurs, known as the 'self-strengtheners', launched a few similar projects in China but they had little impact. The dominant figure at court, the Dowager Empress Cixi, was a conservative whose main concern was to keep the imperial system intact, and, as foreigners from Manchuria, the Qing rulers were increasingly unpopular among their Han subjects.

As China rested on its fading laurels, the ethos of the modernising power across the sea became expansive and aggressive. Japan, the reasoning went, had to enlarge its territorial reach to attain greater economic strength, to absorb its growing population and to spread its message of modernisation through the region. The challenge this posed was not understood in Peking where the Japanese were regarded as culturally inferior 'dwarf bandits' who should simply pay homage to China.

The first dose of reality came in the 1870s when the Japanese occupied the Chinese territory of Taiwan, and Peking had to pay them to withdraw. Then, the two powers clashed in Korea. China regarded the 'Hermit Kingdom' as a client tributary state. However, Japan, moving into the first of the radiating circles of influence envisaged by its policy-makers, backed a rebel faction at the court in Seoul. Both countries sent in troops but then withdrew under a treaty in 1884 that stipulated that neither return to Korea without advance consultations. However, ten years later, the ruler in Seoul called for Chinese help against a peasant rebellion and the Qing obliged. That gave Tokyo good reason to despatch soldiers who took the capital and the palace, installed their own king and had Korea's treaties with China annulled, all in the name of leading the kingdom along the path towards civilisation as defined by Japan.

Faced with this affront, Peking declared war and sent its forces to the northern Korean city of Pyongyang. Though the Qing army was much larger on paper than that fielded by their adversary, it was of poor quality and was routed at Pyongyang. The Japanese then scored a naval victory at the mouth of the Yalu River on the Chinese-Korean frontier and crossed the land border to Manchuria as the defenders fled. The invaders took the strategic centre of Port Arthur (now Lüshunkou District of Dalian) with a skilful manoeuvre and well-organised offensive that enabled them to avoid the strong, German-designed defences.

In a pre-echo of the much bigger massacre they would perpetrate in Nanking 43 years later, the Japanese randomly killed civilians after finding the mutilated heads of some of their captured comrades hanging from the main gate of the fort. 'The town was sacked from end to end and the inhabitants were butchered in their own homes,' an American correspondent wrote. China suffered a further defeat at the important port of Weihaiwei in Shantung after a 23-day battle in freezing temperatures, raging winds and high seas. This victory enabled the Japanese to command the maritime approaches to Peking through the Bohai Bay and to seize ships left at anchor. The Chinese admiral killed himself by drinking poison.

The Qing were in acute peril. Not only had their forces been humiliated but the invaders had a strong army poised to advance on Peking if they so chose. The court called on one of the leading figures of the day, Li Hongzhang, a self-strengthener who had negotiated with foreigners in the past but had been made the scapegoat for earlier defeats. He sailed to negotiate a treaty after Japan occupied the Pescadores Islands off Taiwan. His task was somewhat facilitated by Japanese shame when a nationalist youth wounded him in the face with a pistol shot. Still the peace terms imposed by Tokyo were draconian – the transfer of large territories in northeast China where the population would become Japanese citizens, retention of Taiwan, exclusion of China from Korea, economic concessions and an indemnity as big as the annual imperial budget. This was backed by a threat to send in fifty warships carrying soldiers. China capitulated.

Western powers, alarmed that, as a Russian minister put it, 'the Mikado might become the emperor of China', forced Tokyo to give up its territorial ambitions in Manchuria – though it was compensated with an even larger payment. Having signed the treaty, Li was sent on a lengthy tour to Europe and the United States. China had lost an estimated 35000 men; Japan's official death toll was 969 but was certainly much higher, particularly since a cholera epidemic swept through ships taking troops home – the true total may have been in the region of 17000. The balance of power in East Asia had shifted decisively. 'China's collapse has been terrible… in most heart-breaking, side-bursting fashion,' the Director of the Chinese Customs Service, Robert Hart, observed. Japanese self-confidence soared. As the Qing dynasty weakened despite a short-lived attempt at reform by the emperor which was quashed by the Dowager Cixi, China was forced to give way to another predator, this time from the other side of the globe.[4]

Germany Joins In

The British had been the first to extract concessions from the Qing court in the Treaty of Nanking in 1842 after defeating the imperial navy in the First Opium War. The first of the 'unequal treaties' gave the foreigners independent settlements and trading rights in five Chinese ports which would have their own legal system. They also acquired the island of Hong Kong. The French followed – the Portuguese already occupied Macau.

By the end of the nineteenth century, Germany's highly ambitious Kaiser felt it was high time his nation joined in 'carving up the melon' of China. It gained two concessions, one in the port of Tientsin near Peking and the other in the Yangtze River city of Hankou in central China, where the British, Russians and French were also present. But what Wilhelm really wanted was a naval base from which the power of his Reich could be projected in Asia. 'Hundreds of German merchants will shout with joy in the knowledge that the German empire has at long last set foot firmly in Asia,' he declared. 'Hundreds of thousands of Chinese will shiver if they feel the iron fist of the German empire lying firmly on the neck.'[5]

Grand Admiral Alfred von Tirpitz, the father of the modern German navy, inspected possible sites during a tour of the region in the spring of 1896. After cruising along the China coast, he selected a harbour in Kiaochow Bay on the south side of the Shantung peninsula below the Bohai Bay as an ideal base. Berlin offered to buy it. Peking said it was not for sale. But, soon afterwards, a perfect casus belli appeared when two German Catholic missionaries who were particularly muscular in promoting their religion were murdered in the area at the end of 1897.

Attacks on missionaries had erupted in many parts of China. In Shantung, a traditionally turbulent region which had been the birthplace of Confucius, the European Christians were blamed for a severe drought. Their churches, in the words of one song, had 'bottled up the sky'. The way they threw their support behind converts in village disputes aroused further anger as did their swaggering behaviour.[6]

Though the Foreign Ministry in Berlin urged caution, the Kaiser spotted an ideal opportunity to press German claims in China. 'We must take advantage of this excellent opportunity before another great power either dismembers China or comes to her aid!' he said, 'Now or never!'[7]

The Catholic bishop of Shantung, who was in Germany at the time, hoped that his country would 'use the opportunity to occupy Kiaochow'. He told his ruler that 'it is the last chance for Germany to get possession anywhere in Asia and to firm up our prestige which has dropped… no matter what it costs, we must not under any circumstances give up Kiaochow'. He forecast that it would grow to become 'greater and more meaningful than Shanghai'.[8]

The German minister in Peking, Edmund Heyking, sought any pretext for offence to seek to over-awe the Chinese. On one occasion, he threatened to break off relations after an imperial official pulled his sleeve to try to correct a mistake he made at a ceremony in front of the Chinese ruler; the Chinese duly apologised. To establish the presence of the Reich, Germany's East Asia naval squadron sailed into Kiaochow Bay and marines were landed. In March, 1899, China granted the Reich a 99-year lease on the port and its hinterland.[9]

Emboldened and backed by military force, the missionaries stepped up their activities. Popular resentment spilled over into a movement that spread rapidly through Shantung and became known as the Boxers United in Righteousness. They drew on old secret society rituals, some supposedly conferring invulnerability, practised martial arts and dressed in vivid costumes, declaring their support for the imperial dynasty to free China from the influence of foreigners. In the spring of 1900, they swept out of Shantung and advanced on the capital, attracting adherence as they burnt churches, killed Chinese converts and attacked railways and telegraph lines.

The Boxers surged to Peking where they occupied the inner city around the imperial palace and burned down Christian church buildings in June, 1900. A German diplomat, Baron Clemens von Ketteler, acted in a way his Kaiser would have approved, taking action while the British advised caution. Ketteler instructed the embassy guards to respond to the Boxer destruction, and fighting surged round the German legation. Ketteler, himself, beat up a Chinese civilian and shot a boy dead. Imperial forces in the shape of a unit of Muslim troops from Gansu Province, known as the Kansu Braves, joined in the attack on the foreigners. A Japanese diplomat was killed.

The Empress Cixi, who had decided to accept the Boxers as allies for the dynasty, ordered the foreigners to leave the city by June 20. That morning, Baron Ketteler set out for the Foreign Ministry to discuss the ultimatum. On the way, he ran into imperial troops who shot him in revenge for the killing of the boy. There was a report that one of the soldiers skinned the German and ate his heart.

The drama of the 55-day siege of the Legation Quarter followed, provoking military intervention by a force of 54000 men and 51 ships from Britain, France, Germany, Russia, Italy, Austria, the United States and Japan which contributed the biggest contingent of 20800 troops and 18 vessels. After some stout initial resistance on the road to the capital, the Chinese defences melted away and the dynasty suffered another major setback as the foreigners looted and murdered. Cixi fled with the court and Li Hongzhang was sent to agree to an indemnity of 450 million taels of silver, equivalent to US$6.6 billion in today's value – Russia, which had acquired a concession in Manchuria, took 29 per cent, Germany 20 per cent and Japan only 7.7 per cent. Though the Boxer Protocol did not contain any territorial demands, it was followed by further concessions and a strengthening of the position of foreigners in China.

Home From Home

In Tsingtao, the Germans replicated their home surroundings as much as they could – 6000 miles from the Fatherland behind three mountain ranges at the end of a peninsula stretching into the Yellow Sea. Their postage stamps, featuring ships of various kinds, were denominated in pfennig. Revenue was raised by a 6 per cent land tax instituted by an early governor, Ludwig Schramier, a disciple of the reformer Henry George who was anxious to avoid unfair distribution of land and property speculation. This policy was effective in creating equitable conditions among the colonists and avoiding boom-bust cycles.

By 1913, Tsingtao and its surrounding leased territory contained an estimated 191200 inhabitants, most of them Chinese living in a separate township. The census showed 4470 Europeans and Americans in Tsingtao, 2400 of them German military, plus 316 Japanese. Of the European civilians, 1855 were German, 61 Russian, 51 British and 40 Americans.

Gun batteries aimed out to sea and a string of inland fortifications were designed to repel any Chinese attack. The main barracks was named in honour of Bismarck. The Europeans built gabled, red-roofed villas with flower gardens and deep verandas in the hills overlooking the bay, with 'coolie houses' for the Chinese servants at the back. There was an electricity plant, a modern hospital and nursing and convalescent homes, churches and a waterworks, a horse racing course, beer gardens and an observatory. Eighty million marks were spent on developing the deep-water harbour which needed constant dredging with a man-made horseshoe-shaped breakwater, a kilometre of quays, a dry dock, a 150-ton crane and 1000 Chinese and 50 European staff.[10]

By 1909, 40 miles of metalled roads had been laid down inside the settlement – outside, the tracks were rough and became quagmires when it rained. The Tsingtao brewery provided German-style liquid refreshment. Abundant fresh food was available at the market including delicious grapes. The Germans were keen on fostering education – the German-Chinese High School taught in both languages, charging between 100 and 200 marks a year per pupil with an additional 10 marks a month for boarders; its aim was defined as to be 'the apostle of German culture and science in China and so bring the two people into a closer union'.

At balls in the Governor's mansion, bow-tied men wore formal, three-piece uniforms and the ladies donned long gowns as if they were in Berlin, Hamburg or Munich. Germans and Chinese joined together to celebrate the Kaiser's birthday. Curious locals gathered to watch the Germans in formal dress and uniforms taking meals outside at long trestle tables. The surrounding hills and woods were planted with pine and cypress trees to augment the bamboo groves. There were well-kept, shady woodland roads and paths with views of forest-clad hills and valleys. In the mountains, the Mecklenberg Inn offered traditional German hospitality.

The breeze from the sea kept the temperature down in the early summer and late autumn, attracting holidaymakers from other parts of the country to swim off the Auguste Viktoria Beach with its rows of bathing huts and stroll on the Kaiser Wilhelm Embankment. There were two modern hotels, one of them, the Strand by the sea with rooms for 300 guests, and restaurants and cafes along the shore. Tsingtao became known as 'the Brighton of the East'. As a missionary publication noted in 1912, 'The band of the garrison discourses sweet music on the beach twice a week... and local entertainments are numerous. War vessels and merchantmen and native craft of all descriptions are constantly entering or leaving the port and so an air of bustle and activity is given to the scene. In fact all that makes for recuperating vitality and storing up energy are there in happy combination.'[11]

The concession was under the authority of a naval captain, Clemens Friedrich Meyer-Waldeck, a tall, strongly-built man with a goatee beard who had become governor in 1911. A keen swimmer and horse rider, he exuded quiet authority but also had a sharp temper and was a stickler for detail. Born in 1864, he was married to the daughter of a Prussian officer with whom he had two daughters and a son. His clear abilities meant that he could anticipate promotion after serving his time in Asia.[12]

The Kaiser had always linked German power with business in China and, as *The New York Times* reported in 1903, German commerce and capital engaged in China had increased to 'an extraordinary extent'. Twenty-nine German companies operated in Tsingtao at the start of the twentieth century, using the branch of the Deutsche-Asiatische Bank in a yellow brick building. Trade expanded sevenfold in the first decade of the century, with exports of textiles, silk, vegetable oil, tallow, melons and eggs and imports of yarn, kerosene, metals and sugar. The Shantung Railway Company, with its headquarters in Berlin, ran a line to the provincial capital of Tsinanfu and then Beijing. Its fourteen daily trains carried 640000 passengers and 700000 tons of freight a year but it was never profitable. A private telegraph line linked the port with the capital and four steamships provided a regular connection with Shanghai.

Tsinanfu developed into a thriving township with three broad streets, German shops, a Western-style hotel and a Japanese consulate in a small house in a side street. Two German coal mines in the interior employed 5500 Chinese and 67 Europeans and produced more than 550000 tons of coal between them in 1910; the coal enterprise was taken over by the Shantung Railway Company in 1912 after racking up losses of US$100000. With a fine harbour for his Asian fleet and its prize cruisers, the Scharnhorst and the Gneisenau, and a prosperous settlement that represented the Reich on the other side of the world, the Kaiser could be content.[13]

Rising Chinese nationalism and international complications, especially fear that the British would use their influence to limit German activities elsewhere in China, acted as a brake on the Kaiser's ambitions to extend his country's reach in Shantung outside the settlement. The Foreign Ministry in Berlin, which had always been cautious about China, gained in influence. Still, Tsingtao was a sign that the Reich was able to project its presence on the other side of the world, investing heavily in building what it intended to be a model concession. If it could not rival Britain, Germany figured second among European powers in the world's most populous nation.

Visitors were favourably impressed; one American resident of Japan wrote that 'Germany has shown… that civilization can invade the sleepy and dreamy Orient and be successful. Other Powers have attempted many of the same things in their concessions in the Far East that Germany did in China, but none have really brought the Occident and his ways to Asia, as the Germans did in Kiaochow.'[14]

The Germans were, of course, far from alone in taking advantage of the weakness of the empire and their military strength to develop their presence in China. After the Boxer debacle, the Qing allowed settlements by Austria-Hungary, Belgium and Italy. Britain took a lease on Weihaiwei on the Shantung peninsula where the Japanese had scored a major victory over China. Russia built up its presence in the northeast. Foreign investors moved in as the Qing finally sought to pursue modernisation, notably with the railways that had so enraged the Boxers.

It was Japan that made the biggest imperialist strides. It had held on to Taiwan after the 1894–95 war, and acquired concessions in Tientsin, Hankou, Suzhou and Hangzhou in the east and Chongqing in the west of the country. Its next major victory over Russia in the war of 1904–05 not only burnished its military credentials, especially since this was the first time an Asian country had defeated a European power, but also enabled it to forge out into Manchuria. Japan took over the railways there from its adversary and constructed a formidable industrial-military presence through its lease on the Kwantung Territory and the South Manchuria Railway Zone, which became a regional state-within-a-state that would be the cockpit for expansion by force three decades later.

At the same time, Tokyo reached a web of international agreements starting with a treaty of alliance with Britain signed in 1902 that built on an earlier trade accord. For some in London, the Japanese were 'honorary Europeans' whose modernisation set them apart from other Asians.

Motivated primarily by opposition to Russia, the agreement bound each of the two signatories to remain neutral if the other was involved in war with a single opponent and to come to one another's aid if either was embroiled with more than one other power. The treaty represented a significant step by Britain away from the position of 'splendid isolation' and was a triumph for Japanese politicians who wanted to develop their nation's international reach. It was renewed and expanded in 1905 and 1911. Tokyo also reached understandings with France and the United States and, in 1907, completed the circle with an entente with Russia and a secret agreement to divide Manchuria between them. One outcome was to get acceptance of the occupation of Korea in return for recognition of Western colonial positions in Asia; another was to underline the extent of China's isolation as the enfeebled victim of foreign predators.[15]

On the surface, the Kaiser had nothing to worry about from this scramble for concessions. China was big enough for the European powers each to obtain its own quasi-colonies without bringing down the empire whose weakness suited them so well. Even when the ancient regime finally fell in early 1912 with the announcement of the abdication of the infant last emperor by his mother, the foreigners felt little cause for concern. The republic which succeeded was a weak creature, riven by disputes between regions and military power-brokers. The first President, Sun Yat-sen, gave up the job after three months and was replaced by the military strongman, Yuan Shih-kai, who had served the Qing and then turned against them. He put down an attempted rising backed by Sun and other revolutionaries in 1913 and dissolved parliament at the beginning of the following year taking on sweeping presidential powers for himself. Though the general had an American adviser who thought he should declare himself emperor, the foreigners remained aloof from all this, their concessions unaffected by the change of regime or the swift decline of the Chinese republic. Europe might be entrapped in great power alliances and seething with volatility in the

Balkans but China seemed like a preserved playground, a magic land of infinite possibilities where Western steel ensured supremacy and the Europeans had only to hold together in their islands amid the native masses.

So, on June 12, 1914, the flagship of the British Far Eastern Squadron, the armoured cruiser Minotaur sailed into Tsingtao. On board was Vice Admiral Sir Thomas Martyn Jerram. The British officers dined on the Scharnhorst and danced with German women on the deck of the Gneisenau, as naval historian Robert Massie has recorded. 'The deck was trimmed with bunting, plants and electric lights; the dance floor, set beneath the elevated muzzles of the aft turret guns, was shielded from the night air by heavy canvas curtains; platters of meats, cakes, bread, and butter, and glasses of wine and beer, were spread on the wardroom tables,' he adds. The visitors won a soccer match and their bosses were taken on trips through the hills. But there was an undertone to this 'brotherhood of the sea'. As a German officer noted, 'I do not think we were far wrong in the belief that they desired a little glimpse at our readiness for war.' A British officer was said to have remarked with a smile 'Very nice place, indeed! Two years more and we have it.'[16]

Alone at War

In July, the main ships of Germany's East Asia naval squadron, the Scharnhorst and Guisenau armoured cruisers left Tsingtao for a three-month cruise through the central and southwestern Pacific to show the German flag. The squadron was commanded by Vice Admiral Count Maximilian von Spee, an extremely tall gunnery specialist with a passion for bridge. It was in the Caroline Island, a thousand miles from Tsingtao, when it received news of the assassination of Archduke Franz Ferdinand in Sarajevo and the outbreak of war. Rather than returning to China, Spee decided to sail for Cape Horn and head for Germany across the Atlantic. His ships won a victory over a Royal Navy squadron commanded by Rear-Admiral Sir Christopher Cradock in the Battle of Coronel off Chile in November 1914. But, after reaching the South Atlantic the following month, the German squadron was virtually destroyed when it was confronted by a larger and better armed British force off the Falkland Islands. Spee and his two sons were among the dead. The Gneisenau and the Scharnhorst were both sunk. Of the eight German vessels, only two escaped; one, the light cruiser Dresden, was scuttled by her captain after an encounter with a British squadron in mid-March 1915.

Tsingtao's naval force was further weakened when the light cruiser, the Emden, took to sea to avoid being bottled up in the harbour – it evaded British ships sent to track it down and became a highly effective harrier of shipping in Asian waters in the following months. In the harbour were a torpedo boat, S-90, four gunboats – the Iltis, Jaguar, Tiger, and Luchs – and an Austro-Hungarian cruiser, the Kaiserin Elisabeth. On land, the German forces consisted of around 1500 men grouped in four foot companies, a 140-strong mounted company, a field artillery battery with six quick-firing 7.7 centimetre cannons, 108 military engineers and two horse-drawn machine-gun detachments. Another 180 civilians in the settlement could be called up. There were also two yellow observation balloons and two Rumpler Taube aircraft, Germany's first mass-produced military plane with long, bat-like wings and a linen covering that rendered it virtually invisible when flying above 1200 feet.

The balloons were not much use since there was no good mooring place that would enable those aboard to get a general view of the concession. One of the planes was wrecked when it crashed on its first flight, severely injuring the pilot. The other was more successful and its flier, Lieutenant Gunther Plüschow, became a star of the siege, famed for his courage and self-confidence.[17]

The German troops had carried out a war game the previous year and a precautionary plan had been drawn up to requisition civilian craft for military use and to stockpile supplies. A troopship had arrived with fresh men as part of the regular rotation of forces. Governor Meyer-Waldeck summoned help from other German units in China notably a naval detachment of some 750 men from Tientsin commanded by Lieutenant Colonel Paul Kuhlo, a hulking figure more than 6 feet tall and weighing 250 pounds known for his combination of good humour and meticulousness.

The settlement was far beyond any help the Kaiser could send apart from his message of support. It had a natural defence line along the hills and mountains of the Kaiserstuhl and the Litsuner Heights which lay between it and the rest of the province. But railway and telegraph communications could easily be cut. Its isolation was underlined when a 12000-ton British warship, the Triumph, sailed from Hong Kong to patrol the coast off Shantung, capturing and sinking a merchant ship carrying 1800 tons of coal for the Germans. A study of the defences found that artillery shells were in short supply and the approach of war set off a run on the Deutsche-Asiatische Bank which had to post guards as cash was brought in from branches elsewhere in eastern China. Holidaymakers hurried home. The Governor told the British living in Tsingtao that they could remain 'if they will give their word of honour through the British Consul not to engage in any act which may be regarded as inimical to the German Empire' but they and the thirty French residents left. So did the families of the rank-and-file soldiers; the wives of officers remained to act as nurses.[18]

The rain started to fall on July 31, 'the rooms are all wet, water is running down the wall, drops from the ceiling,' an artillery man recorded in his diary. Mosquitoes swarmed. The downpour damaged the telegraph lines. Tracks outside the metalled roads of the settlement became virtually impassable.[19]

Governor Meyer-Waldeck declared martial law on August 1. Security precautions were increased. Infantrymen occupied redoubts on the edges of the settlement. Troops dug fortifications and laid mines. The white uniforms worn by some of the soldiers were dyed green or blue. German soldiers posted elsewhere in China were summoned to join the defence of Tsingtao along with reservists. But the Governor was not too worried for the time being – Russia had declared war but was fully occupied in Manchuria. The two powers which might cause him trouble, Britain and Japan, had not committed themselves.

That began to change on August 4 when Britain declared war but the vital decision lay in Tokyo. A British military planning report drawn up in 1913 had made clear that, on its own, the UK would not be able to mount an attack for some time. Ten thousand troops would be required, shipped from India in fifteen vessels, it calculated, naval supremacy would have had to have been established in the region. A surprise attack was ruled out.[20]

With the German East Asia squadron at large and the Emden poised to play a hunter role in the region, British planners felt they could not contain the enemy on their own and turned to their Asian ally which had built up a fleet of 113 naval ships including a strong force of cruisers. Anglo-Japanese relations were at a low ebb, largely because of London's concern at Tokyo's ambitions in China which it saw as affecting British interests. But the approach for help at sea in Asia met with a positive response and the Foreign Office asked Japan to deploy warships for 'hunting out and destroying German armed merchantmen in China.'

The request given to the Japanese ambassador in London on August 7 added that, 'Such an action on the part of Japan will constitute a declaration of war with Germany, but it is difficult to see how such a step is to be avoided.' At 10 p.m. that day, the Japanese Cabinet met. The Foreign Minister, Katō Takaaki, who had previously been ambassador to Britain, argued that complying with the request would be in accordance with the alliance with the UK and would also serve to raise his country's role in East Asia. At 2 a.m., the cabinet adjourned and Katō went to report to the Emperor. When the ministers assembled again later in the day, the decision was to send an ultimatum to Germany demanding it hand over Tsingtao.

Katō's decisive approach upset British plans that Japan should merely play a supportive role. A suggestion by the Foreign Office that France and Russia should also be asked to join in the attack on Tsingtao in order to give it the character of a pan-Allied initiative was ignored by the Japanese. For Katō and his colleagues this was not so much an attack on Germany under the alliance with Britain as a means of enlarging their country's position in China.

As in 1894–95 and 1904–05, Tokyo was anxious to exploit what it saw as its destiny, in its second armed confrontation with a European power. That alarmed China, Australia and New Zealand which had no wish to see an expansion of Japanese power. But, having invoked support from its ally, the Foreign Office in London could not rein it in. To bolster its case, the government in Tokyo leaked an account of a meeting with the German ambassador at which he was said to have flown into a rage and to have used threatening language.

Katō and his colleagues rejected British attempts to set limits on its action and drew up the ultimatum on its own at an imperial conference, handing it to the German envoy in the evening of August 15. It demanded that the Reich withdraw all its armed vessels from East Asia waters and hand over the leased territory of Kiaochow which would 'eventually' be returned to China. Berlin was given seven days to respond. Two decades after its military triumph over imperial China, Japan had defied British policy and taken a fresh step towards its aim of becoming the leading power in the Far East.

The German ambassador made evident his country's response to the ultimatum by packing to go home. When the deadline was reached at noon on August 23, an imperial decree from the palace in Tokyo announced: 'We hereby declare war against Germany and We command Our Army and Navy to carry on hostilities against that Empire with all their strength... Germany is, at Kiaochow, its leased territory in China, busy with war-like preparations, while its armed vessels cruising the seas of Eastern Asia are threatening Our commerce and that of Our Ally. The peace of the Far East is in jeopardy.'

The Japanese fleet sailed to begin the blockade while its army massed troops to stage a landing, with the United Kingdom reduced to a subordinate role. Sir

Edward Grey, the Foreign Secretary, told the embassy in Tokyo that British forces in the Far East would coordinate with the Japanese – when the latter wanted to. A brigade of British and Indian troops pulled together in India to join the attack was placed under Japanese command. Its commander, Colonel Nathaniel Barnardiston, asked for his unit to be given independent status, but was told that it would be subordinate to the Asian ally.[21]

The government in Tokyo said that Japan's object was 'to eliminate from the continent of China the root of the German influence which forms a constant menace to the peace of the Far East and thus to secure the aim of the alliance with Great Britain. She harbours no design for territorial aggrandizement nor entrains any desire to promote any other selfish end.' German diplomats in China reacted by wondering how their presence in Shantung threatened peace in the region, and pointed to Russia as the nation Japan should be worried about.[22]

In all this, nobody bothered to consult the administration in Peking led by Yuan Shih-kai, which proclaimed its neutrality in the conflict between the European powers and wanted to avoid any clash with Japan. Knowing how difficult Tsingtao would be to defend, the Germans tried to hand it back to China as Japanese troops prepared to sail from Nagasaki and contacted Washington to try to get a declaration that foreign settlements in China would be regarded as neutral territory.

But pressure from Tokyo forestalled this. China simply annulled the lease when Japan's ultimatum ran out, leaving the territory hanging in the air – it was no longer legally Germany but Japan's action meant China could not regain it. Tokyo advised the Chinese that it was obliged to act 'for the assurance of peace of the Far East and the preservation of China's territorial integrity and the maintenance of peace and order in the same country.' By the logic of the concessions, one foreign power abrogated to itself the right to use force to take over the settlement granted to another foreign power in order to safeguard China's territorial integrity.[23]

That pointed to a longer-term outcome foreshadowed in a note sent by Grey to the ambassador in Tokyo, Sir Conyngham Greene, telling him what the Foreign Secretary was about to tell Japan's envoy to London: 'After this war, if Germany was beaten, France, Russia and ourselves would naturally get compensation in parts of the world other than China. The only compensation that Japan would get would be in the region of China. It would therefore be unfair for any of us to put forward claims depriving Japan of compensation for the blood and treasure she might have to spend.'

Realpolitik reigned, at the expense of China. The Siege of Tsingtao would thus contribute to the evolution of a much vaster conflict in the decades ahead, with its present-day heritage.[24]

Battle

Japan's choice of a landing site for the force sent to take Tsingtao showed the hollowness of its claim that it sought no territorial aggrandisement and wanted only to protect the integrity of China. Instead of heading for the southern shores of the peninsula, the Japanese went ashore in the north on September 2 and marched overland, occupying towns and the railway as they went. If Tsingtao was their main objective, they were making sure they gained as much influence as possible on the ground beforehand, in disregard of Chinese efforts to limit the area affected by the fighting and to maintain neutrality.

At the headquarters they set up in the provincial capital of Tsinanfu, the officers consulted a map of the whole of Shantung, not just the Kiaochow area. In Europe, Britain expressed outrage at Germany's violation of Belgian neutrality, but no such scruples applied to China. When the British consul in Tsinanfu, John Pratt, expressed his indignation in strong language he was reprimanded by his country's Minister in Peking.

At a meeting of the Council of State in Peking, one councillor, Liang Chi Chao, noted Japan's violation of the neutral zone decreed by the Republic outside the borders of the German settlement and asked rhetorically if there were any German soldiers there. 'They are trying to occupy the whole of Shantung Province which they will turn into another Manchuria.' A fellow Council member, Chen Kuo Hsiang, asked, 'If Japan takes Shantung, what will become of the nation?' while a general said, 'Apparently, Japan can seize anything it wants as a prize of war. This must be stopped.'

A protest lodged with Japan only brought a warning that the advancing troops would take the whole of the railway that connected to the provincial capital; any opposition by the Chinese would be regarded as 'an act unfriendly to Japan and partial to Germany.' China was forced to accept the fait accompli. Its troops offered no resistance as the Japanese advanced well outside the Kiaochow zone through the countryside of poor villages, pines and willows.[25]

The main Japanese land force was the 18th Infantry Division with 23000 soldiers including a cavalry unit, which led the attack on the railway line, and 142 artillery pieces. They came ashore in an area on the north of the peninsula which a British officer attached to the force recorded as 'not a very suitable place for disembarkation of troops owing to the shallow water near shore which made it impossible for the transports to approach closer than 2 to 5 miles from the beach.' The soldiers were ferried fourteen at a time in small sampans with their guns in two crafts, lashed together. Steam launches carried the cavalry horses to land. Storms disrupted the operation, swamping sampans and putting the landing eleven days behind schedule.

Floods from the heavy rain impeded the move inland. The vanguard of the advance was cut off at one point by the flooding. Still they achieved their objective of taking towns and the rail line as they moved towards Tsingtao, doing all they could to mask their progress censoring local post and telegraph communications and barring foreigners from their march route.[26]

In Tsingtao, the Governor, who established his command post in a concrete basement in the Bismarck barracks, ordered the defences to be strengthened, sending Colonel Kuhlo and his men into the hills to dig entrenchments, construct artillery positions, lay mines and put up lines of barbed wire; initially, they used Chinese labourers but, as news of the Japanese advance reached them, the local people melted away. Knowing the chances of being overrun, Kuhlo made sure the positions being built had escape routes.[27]

The Germans were cheered by news of their fellow countrymen's victories in Europe and were indignant at the ultimatum from Japan to quit Tsingtao. 'They can tell this to a Russian but not to a German,' one wrote in his diary. They grew bored awaiting the arrival of the enemy though there was some excitement when a Japanese plane flew overhead and dropped four bombs that caused no damage.

On September 7, the diary writer, whose name is not recorded, wrote: 'Everyone is breathing with relief, at last they are coming. Now it will end in God's hands.' But then four days of inaction followed. 'One only hopes that soon something will happen, either the Japanese win or we are defeated or (sic) or the other way round. The first will probably prove correct for us, for the idea that our 10000 men can hold for long against 1 to 15 times that number is difficult to accept… Still, however, we hope that the Japanese attack us, for it is for this reason that we are soldiers.' The Kaiser was deeply concerned about the fate of Tsingtao saying with typical hyperbole, or perhaps simply the racism of the epoch, that 'it would shame me more to surrender Tsingtao to the Japanese than Berlin to the Russians.' [28]

There was sporadic activity. Lieutenant Plüschow flew his reconnaissance plane to detect the enemy position, keeping high enough to avoid fire from the ground. A Japanese was found trying to poison the water supply with typhus bacilli, and was promptly shot. Japanese aircraft dropped bombs but did no damage. In what was the first recorded air-sea battle, a Japanese seaplane unsuccessfully attacked the German ships, the Kaiserin Elisabeth and the Jaguar, in the bay with bombs. [29]

A second Japanese landing was staged on September 18 in the south of the peninsula 18 miles from Tsingtao. The 1650-strong contingent of British troops from the South Wales Borderers and 500 Sikhs who brought with them a troop of mules joined them four days later. They had travelled from Tientsin in hired Chinese transport ships escorted by HMS Triumph and a torpedo boat and accompanied by a vessel chartered to serve as a floating hospital. Progress towards Tsingtao was slow because of the state of the roads and the clog of Japanese transport vehicles, guns and soldiers.

'Every valley becomes a torrent and every road or track a mass of deep mud,' the British commander, Nathaniel Barnardiston, who had been given the temporary rank of Brigadier General, recorded. His men, in their tropical shorts and solar topees, were soaked by the constant downpour as they struggled up to their knees in mud into which their equipment sank.[30]

On September 27, Barnardiston went to meet the Japanese commander, General Kamio. A journalist who called at his headquarters in a cottage during the advance on Tsingtao described him as 'short, sturdily built of about 55 with a closely-cut, grey moustache partially concealing full lips held firm by a square, slightly projecting chin. The black peak of his flat khaki cap, with its red band and five pointed stars, comes well down over alert intelligent eyes. His coat and riding breeches are of khaki coloured mouse grey, and black leather top-boots come up over his knees. A shoulder strap almost entirely gold with two gold stars are all his ornaments. The dull gold buttons of his coat or tunic are almost the same as common soldiers. His staff, as highly trained a body of men as one could find, are within half a minute's walk of him. In a small room, lit by a couple of lamps, the closing hours of the day find them still busy, heads bent over broad maps.'[31]

A British major attached to the Japanese headquarters described Kamio as 'of a somewhat reserved disposition and a calm temperament' who was credited with being an officer likely to be cautious in his plans of operations. Kamio had been military attaché in Peking in the 1890s and took part in the Japanese offensives in northern China. His chief of staff had been a staff officer during the war with Russia and was then attached to the German army. He served as military attaché in Berlin and attended manoeuvres in Lorraine in 1908. At one point, he was jeered at, an insult he never forgave. [32]

Relations between the two allies were not good on land though they remained cordial among the two fleets. With 30000 men and the supreme command, the Japanese saw no reason to take the British into their confidence about their plans or to associate them with messages to the enemy. After one dispute which was referred to their respective governments, Kamio banished any lingering British doubts about who was in charge by signing himself 'Commander in Chief of the Army Besieging Tsingtao'.[33]

The Japanese did not have a high opinion of the Borderers though they seem to have thought better of the Sikhs. They resented having to divert part of their supplies to the British whom they sometimes took for Germans, firing at them and blocking their movements; in the end, the British had to wear special identifying markings and employ interpreters. According to a British diplomat in Tientsin, Japanese officers told the Chinese that their allies 'are not good fighters and that their officers come from wealthy families and are therefore unfitted for the hardships and dangers of a campaign.'[34]

The Japanese established their headquarters in a square position in a valley. Nine narrow lanes ran between the tents and stone houses which had thatched roofs, mud floors, paper over the windows and brick *kang* beds heated from below. The horses were kept in a paddock together with carts, wagons and gun carriages. The names of the lanes were marked on strips of white paper – Line of Communications Street, Sergeants'

Street, Interpreters' Street. Breakfast was taken from 6 to 7, lunch from 12 to 1 and supper from 5 to 6. To boost morale, the Emperor and Empress sent in an aide-de-camp with their good wishes, 5000 cigarettes stamped with the imperial monogram and, for the officers, five bottles of sake.[35]

The terrible weather and the bad condition of the roads, as well as Kamio's circumspection and uncertainty as to the strength of the defences, meant that the Japanese-British force spent weeks putting the town under siege before starting its assault. The rain fell continuously. Horses and men were plastered with mud which clogged the wheels of their vehicles as animals strained forward and their drivers cracked the whip. The British had a hard time brewing up tea over sputtering pine logs. Their pipes went out even if the bowls were turned downward. Streams of water suddenly widened to a breadth of 5 or 6 yards. There was little shelter since most of the few houses in the hills had been damaged and lacked roofs.[36]

At the end of September, the ships on both sides brought their guns to bear to augment the land artillery. But all the sound and fury had little effect. A German kitchen at the Bismarck barracks was hit but the cook escaped. A pigsty was destroyed by a direct hit together with its Chinese keeper. Bodies flew in the air when a shell landed in a cemetery where Russian sailors had been buried after putting in at Tsingtao during the war with Japan.[37]

Before the Allies launched their planned attack on the outer defences, the Germans fell back from their forward positions. The defenders had reason to cheer when the Jaguar gunboat sank a light Japanese warship in the bay. But the Japanese took a peak known as the Eagle's Nest which commanded a view across the town. There was no hiding the predicament of the defenders as the far superior Allied forces closed in with a numerical advantage of six to one and far more artillery. A mass grave was dug; an officer jumped into it and addressed his men: 'Drive the thoughts of seeing Father or Mother out of your heads, We cannot obtain victory here; only die. Still, before it reaches that point, take as many of the yellow Apes with you as you can. A last thought for home; Hip, Hip, Hurra!'[38]

In early October, the Germans fell back from their forward positions, burning the Mecklenberg Inn and destroying bridges over the mountain gorges. As Japanese surveillance planes flew overhead, Meyer-Waldeck concentrated on two lines of defence along the ridges closest to the settlement, German warships bombarded the Allied positions while mines sank three Japanese steamers and, on October 17, a cruiser. Japanese artillery damaged the German gunboat, Iltis, but the German torpedo boat S-90 sank the Japanese cruiser Takachiho with the loss of 271 officers and men; the SS-90 was unable to make it back to harbour for lack of fuel and had to be scuttled. Inland, the Japanese fortified their positions in Tsinan and other Chinese centres and took over the railway rolling stock. Traffic on the railway line halted; the resulting demand for carts sent their price up by 50 per cent.[39]

The defenders staged a night attack in the middle of the month but were repulsed. Some of the heaviest fighting then took place in mid-October as the Japanese and British attacked the German front line where the defenders were augmented by cavalry and fired more than 1500 shells a day. At the request of Governor Meyer-Waldeck, there was a short ceasefire for the dead to be collected from the battlefield. Some were left behind – as the attackers advanced, they came across a trench containing twenty-eight German corpses. [40]

The Japanese scored an important advance by taking the Kushan-Prince Henry hills on October 17. Their horses dragged 100 siege guns with 1200 shells each on to the heights where an observation post was erected. Lieutenant Plüschow flew over each morning to observe their progress but there was nothing the defenders could do to stop them. At sea, the torpedo boat, S-90, which had been sent out with an order to attack any enemy ships it came across, blew apart an old Japanese cruiser killing 253 of those on board; then, fearing that he would be tracked down by a big naval force and would be unable to regain Tsingtao, the German captain scuttled his vessel when it ran out of fuel.

Japanese planes flew on bombing raids under a full moon but did little damage. After a delay caused by a fresh storm, the general shelling of Tsingtao started at 6.10 a.m. on October 31. 'Gentlemen, the show has started,' a British officer remarked to a group of observers on the Prince Heinrich Berg, as he raised his binoculars. Guided by Plüschow's observation flights, the Germans returned fire but the attackers had a clear numerical artillery advantage and the defenders were running short of shells.

One of this group, Jefferson Jones, an American living in Japan who had gained an invitation to accompany the troops, heard 'a continuous rumble as if a giant bowling alley were in use'. 'There was the theatre of war laid out before us like a map,' Jones wrote. 'To the left were the Japanese and British cruisers in the Yellow Sea, preparing for the bombardment of Tsingtao. Below was a Japanese battery, stationed near the Mecker House, which the Germans had burned in their retreat from the mountains. Directly ahead was the city of Tsingtao with the Austrian cruiser Kaiserin Elisabeth steaming about in the harbour, while to the right one could see the German coast and central forts and redoubts and the entrenched Japanese and British camps... Everywhere the valley at the rear of Tsingtao was alive with golden flashes or the flashing from discharging guns, and at the same time great clouds of bluish-white smoke would suddenly spring up around the German batteries where some Japanese shells had burst.'[41]

The Japanese shelling was extremely accurate – 'You couldn't wish for better shooting,' a British officer told the correspondent of the *North China Daily News*. 'It's first class.' At midnight on the second day of the bombardment, the journalist listened to 'the rapid, drum-like roll of pompoms and maxims broken into and drowned by the deep thud of heavier guns. Every now and then, there are flashes of red in the sky.' The shells devastated German forts and redoubts dug into the hills, and set fire to coal stores and the Standard Oil and Asiatic Petroleum tanks at the docks. The 150-ton crane at the harbour was brought down. The captain of the Austrian cruiser fired her last shells and then had the ship stripped of useful equipment before murmuring 'Addio Lisa' and scuttling her.[42]

The bombardment went on for a week after which the allied infantry moved forward on a narrow front in four sections starting 5000 yards from the defensive line. Some of the Japanese infantry advanced slowly in parallel lines of trenches they dug as they went. Others dug shelters in the hillside, covering them with branches.

Barnardiston established British headquarters in a

pretty green gully with slender pines. German artillery fire was inaccurate and did little damage; as the shells landed at a safe distance, British troops sang 'You made me love you'. But eight Welsh troops were killed and twenty-four wounded as working parties laid a pontoon across a river bed.

When they reached the first redoubts on the hills, the attackers found that the defenders had abandoned them. Elsewhere, the Germans hunkered down in the relative safety of their positions, not putting their heads over the parapets to return fire. Some of the defenders were captured. A British officer saw one group of sixty 'with heads sunk forward on breast... their dejection was far from pleasant to watch. They were brave men, they had done their best, their clothes were ragged. They seemed amazed to see Britons standing by and, as though with final effort, they raised their heads as they passed and met me eye to eye with burning looks.'[43]

Meyer-Waldeck quickly came to the conclusion that resistance was futile despite a message from the Kaiser assuring the defenders that, 'With me, the entire Germanic nation looks with pride on the heroes of Tsingtao whom, true to the word of the Governor, are fulfilling their duties. You should know all of my appreciation.'

After a night-time artillery exchange and an early-morning attack by a Japanese storming party on the central defence line which took 200 prisoners, the allies staged a general attack. 'The noise of the final assault was as if the hills were being flogged with gigantic iron rods,' the *North China Daily News* correspondent wrote. The shelling had churned up great heaps of mud and stone, burying men in some places. Some of the defenders blew up their positions before retreating into the town.[44]

There were pools of blood on the parapets of the redoubts. Japanese Red Cross workers moved about with stretchers. The correspondent saw 'a man with a face unrecognizable, another with legs torn away, a third in a heap too mangled to look at.' Germans blew up their forts as defeat came ever closer. A Japanese officer stood under his national flag on top of a captured redoubt 'laughing like a schoolboy after a huge prank'. He picked up a German officer's sword and handed it to the journalist crying 'Pour mémoire' and cackling hoarsely.

In Redoubt Number Nine, there were bodies blown to bits amidst a litter of coats, leggings, straps, papers, clocks, thermometers and brushes. Japanese planes flew over the town saying that it would be 'against the will of God as well as against humanity' if the defenders destroyed weapons and ships. As the attackers switched from high-explosive shells to shrapnel, the Germans were in chaos, their communications cut, many of their guns out of action, their trench lines and barbed wire defences breached. In his tent behind the lines, General Kamio sat placidly smoking a cigar and coaxing his parrot to take breakfast, telephones ringing around him.[45]

Lieutenant Plüschow, who dropped bombs on the attackers and claimed to have brought down one Japanese plane with pistol shots, was nearly hit by fire from the ground during one of his reconnaissance flights and headed off inland. He had with him the Governor's final dispatch. After covering 150 miles, he crashed into a rice paddy, and made his way by foot, boat and rail to Shanghai where he procured Swiss travel documents and sailed for Nagasaki, Honolulu, and San Francisco, crossing the US to New York where he met a friend who got him on to a ship bound for Italy. However, bad weather forced it to put in at Gibraltar, where the British arrested him and sent him to a prisoner-of-war camp in Leicestershire from which he promptly escaped. After hiding in London, he finally reached Germany, only to be arrested as a spy before his true identity became known and he was feted as 'the hero from Tsingtao', going on to serve in occupied Latvia and write a bestselling book about his experiences before embarking on explorations of Patagonia where he crashed his plane and died in 1931.

Some of the German officers argued for a last ditch defence house by house, but Meyer-Waldeck ordered the truce flag to be raised at 6.30 a.m. on November

7. 'Since my defensive means are exhausted, I am now ready to enter into surrender negotiations for the now open city,' he wrote in a message to Kamio. Japanese soldiers dropped to the ground and slept. German prisoners stood in groups watched by guards. 'Some sulked, others chatted and laughed. Three or four were drunk,' the *North China Daily News* correspondent wrote.

The British marched into the town ahead of the Japanese, four abreast whistling 'Everybody's Doing it'. As they passed, Germans turned their backs and bent down to show their buttocks to their fellow Europeans who had allied with Asians to fight against them. The British then congregated in a big warehouse at the docks where bread, milk and tins of butter and jam were laid out on long tables. Two of them who went out for a walk were killed by a German shell fired by a defender who was not ready to give up. Surrender negotiations were held that afternoon. They demanded that all German military personnel would become prisoners of war and all German equipment would be theirs. The agreement was discussed and, after the Germans had agreed to the terms, signed by the German and Japanese chiefs of staff and a Japanese naval officer. The British were not consulted or asked to put their name to the document.

After the Allies formally took possession of the settlement on November 16, a representative of the Emperor, wearing a tail coat, knickerbockers and yellow shoes handed the British troops a parchment from his ruler expressing pleasure at their participation in the battle, plus a consignment of cigarettes with the imperial chrysanthemum crest. Kamio held a banquet for the British officers, but their contingent was lost in the mass of Japanese troops in the victory parade. Though Barnardiston was subsequently received with considerable pomp in Tokyo, including a dinner given by the Emperor, the British Embassy was handed a note that it would be 'more convenient for practical purposes' if they left matters to Kamio and his men.[46]

A Japanese governor was appointed and Tokyo made plain that it was not going to hand over the territory to China. The Japanese put their casualties in the fighting on land at 236 dead and 1282 wounded. The British suffered 12 killed and 53 wounded. The German dead numbered 199 with 504 wounded – the dead were buried in Tsingtao while most of the surviving troops were taken to a detention camp at the foot of the Prince Heinrich Berg though the officers were allowed to remain at liberty in the town, before they were all shipped to prisoner-of-war camps in Japan.

The Spoils of Victory

At a time of Allied retreats in Europe, the outcome of the small battle in the East was decidedly good news. 'The heaviest blow delivered at German world-power has been at the hands of Japan by the capture of Tsingtao and, although her sphere of action has been limited, it has provided the Allies with a prize that, in the eyes of Germany, is the greatest that has been won from her since the war began,' a British Cabinet note declared. As the official *British History of the Great War* put it, 'Thus three months after the war began, Far Eastern Waters were permanently barred to the enemy and the Japanese were free to take their place in the world-wide combination that had been designed in Whitehall.' [47]

What that meant for Tokyo became all too clear two months later when Yuan Shih-kai was presented with a list of twenty-one demands drawn up by Prime Minister Ōkuma Shigenobu and Foreign Minister Katō Takaaki and approved by the Emperor. These began by confirming the position Japan had obtained by military force and asserted its control of railways, coasts and major cities of Shantung. They went on to expand the Japanese sphere of influence in Manchuria and Inner Mongolia. China was to be barred from extending concessions to countries other than Japan. Going beyond territorial claims, a final set of demands called for the appointment of Japanese advisers to the government in Peking and to the police force.

The demands were to be kept secret and there would be serious consequences if they were not met, Tokyo warned. To drive home the threat, they were written on paper with a watermark of battleships and machine guns. Peking rejected them and leaked the contents to the Western powers in the hope of support given the implications for their own positions in China. When this was not forthcoming, Yuan negotiated a new set of demands with Tokyo which reduced the total to thirteen.

A treaty was signed on May 25, 1915. The extent to which Yuan really opposed Japanese expansion in his own country is a moot point. An extremely wily politician with few if any principles, he was plotting to declare himself emperor, which happened at the end of 1915, and may have wanted to win Tokyo's support in his march to the throne (which did not last for long as opposition from major provinces obliged him to step down and he died the following year).

Britain and the United States were both alarmed by the extent of Japan's ambitions – Washington, which held to the Open Door Policy by which all powers should be equal in China, recognised Tokyo's 'special interests' in Manchuria, Mongolia and Shantung but expressed concern over further infringements of Chinese sovereignty while London worried about Japanese attempts to turn China into a protectorate.

Still, as so often is the case, concern did not translate into pre-emptive action especially when Britain found it necessary to appeal for the despatch of Japanese warships to fight in the Mediterranean. When Tokyo agreed to send vessels to Malta, the Foreign Office responded that, 'His Majesty's Government accede with pleasure to the request of the Japanese Government for an assurance that they will support Japan's claims in regard to disposal of Germany's rights in Shantung.' A secret treaty to this effect that also split German islands in the Pacific between the two powers was signed in February, 1917. France, Italy and Russia then reached similar understandings. China did not help itself by a secret exchange pressed on it by Japan in 1918 in which it 'gladly agreed' to a note acknowledging the other power's interests in Shantung.

China's decision to declare war on Germany in August, 1917, made no difference. Nor did the 100000

Chinese who had gone to France to dig trenches for the Allies, freeing soldiers to fight; some of the labourers died from shelling or disease but they were soon forgotten by the victors (One can still visit Chinese cemeteries in northern France). Five years after the fall of the Qing, the country was descending into a decade of warlord anarchy but the Foreign Ministry continued to function in Peking and, foreseeing the defeat of the Reich, its diplomats calculated that the declaration would enable them to reclaim the concessions they had given to the European powers. But Tokyo was intent on expanding its influence under a Monroe Doctrine of its own in East Asia, and counted on the secret treaty of 1917 to bolster its claims. To advance its case, it paid a 20 million yen bribe to the main warlord in northern China to side with it over Shantung.

As they went to the Paris Peace Conference of 1919, the Japanese knew that world opinion was hostile to their retention of Shantung. President Woodrow Wilson described the treaty, which had been revealed to the Allies, as a private arrangement which he did not recognise. The British Prime Minister, David Lloyd George, assured Japan that a promise was a promise but the undertaking had been only to support Tokyo's claims not to guarantee that they would succeed. Japan suffered a defeat at the conference on another of its main demands for mention of racial equality to be included in the charter of the League of Nations; the issue was deeply troubling for the President of a party with strong support in the southern states and, when the Japanese gained a majority in their favour, he was reduced to decreeing it 'not adopted' because the vote had not been unanimous.

China, which had greeted news of the Allied victory with a three-day public holiday and a celebratory march of 60000 people through Peking, had high hopes for the peace conference. It had ended up by declaring war on Germany in 1917 and had sent a large number of labourers to help the efforts on the Western front. Before embarking for Paris, its delegates talked on getting all the unequal treaties abrogated to regain the concessions along with national control of railways and tariffs that had been ceded to foreigners. But the sixty-strong Chinese delegation, which lodged at the Lutetia Hotel on the Left Bank in the French capital, was split between representatives of the various factions in the country and its nominal leader, Lu Zhengxiang, who had been educated at a Western school in Shanghai and married a Belgian. He disappeared during the final stages of the conference. In later years, he became abbot of the Benedictine Monastery in Belgium and was buried in Bruges.

However, they had the sympathy of the Americans led by Robert Lansing, the Secretary of State, who said he had gone to Paris 'to have it out once and for all with

Japan' which he took to calling 'Prussia'. The US delegation helped the Chinese delegation and was impressed by a young diplomat, Wellington Koo, a Columbia University graduate whose eloquence contrasted to the wooden performances of the Japanese. The perspicacious American ambassador to China, Paul Reinsch, warned that, 'Should Japan be given a freer hand and should anything be done which could be interpreted as a recognition of the special position of Japan, either in the form of a so-called Monroe Doctrine or in any other way, forces will be set in action which make a huge armed conflict absolutely inevitable within one generation.'[48]

The British fretted about the menace Japanese expansion would pose to their position in China and Tokyo's general attitude with the unconcealed contempt for the performance of Barnardiston's men at Tsingtao was a further irritant. 'Today we have come to know Japan – the real Japan – is a frankly opportunistic, not to say selfish, country, of very moderate importance compared with the giants of the Great War, but with a very exaggerated opinion of her role in the universe,' the ambassador in Tokyo wrote.[49]

But the Japanese dug in their heels. Having conceded defeat on the racial equality issue, they could not suffer a second reverse. So they warned that, if they were baulked on Shantung, they would walk out of the conference. This would have been catastrophic since Italy had quit the talks after failing to get what it wanted over the territory of Fiume in the Adriatic. Their strongest card was simply that, whatever they said about national rights, the priority for other participants when the issue came up for determination in the hectic final days of the meeting, was to produce an overall agreement and, for Wilson in particular, to launch the League of Nations.

The sorry history of China since the middle of the previous century made it that much easier for the statesmen gathered at the Quai d'Orsay to close their eyes to this blatant reward for aggression which ran counter to the principles the League was meant to embody. As Lord Curzon, who replaced Balfour as Foreign Secretary, put it: 'Within sight of their [Japan's] shores, you have the great helpless, hopeless, and inert mass of China, one of the most densely populated countries in the world, utterly deficient in cohesion or strength, engaged in perpetual conflict between the North and the South, destitute of military capacity or ardour, an easy prey.'[50]

Wilson changed tack to side with Lloyd George on the sanctity of treaties, even secret ones. That included the agreement between Beijing and Tokyo on Shantung. Koo got nowhere with a warning which echoed Reinsch to the effect that 'it is a question of whether we can guarantee a peace of half a century to the Far East or if a situation will be created which can lead to war within ten years.' On the last morning of the conference, the three major allied powers could not risk Japan reacting to disappointment over Tsingtao by making an embarrassing scene over the racial equality decision or, even worse, walking out. 'If Italy remains away and Japan goes home, what becomes of the League of Nations?' Wilson replied when his press secretary told him that world opinion backed China.[51]

So Japan emerged with a satisfactory result. The President, who said he had not slept the previous night for worrying about China, explained to the media that the settlement was 'as satisfactory as could be got out of the tangle of treaties in which China herself was involved'. He also conjured up the notion that, if Japan left the meeting, it would conclude a military alliance with Russia and Germany. 'I know that I shall be accused of violating my own principles. Yet nevertheless I must work for world order and organisation and against anarchy and a return to the old militarism,' he explained, as if handing over Chinese territory as a result of armed action by Japan was a step likely to promote order and decrease militarism.[52]

There was a proviso. Wilson's rhetoric about national self-determination and British concerns about the impact of Japanese expansion on its interests in China meant that Tokyo had to agree 'to hand the Shantung peninsula in full sovereignty to China, retaining only the economic privileges granted to Germany and the right to establish a settlement under the usual conditions at Tsingtao'. But this was quite meaningless since no date was set and the 'economic privileges' were taken to cover the railway to Tsinan, mining and telegraph rights plus all German state property. 'For the sake of greater unity in the pressure that is brought to bear on Germany and for the sake of the unborn League of Nations, China, an ally, is surrendered to Japan and is thrown on her mercy under no better pledge of good treatment than Japan's word for it,' as the *Far Eastern Review* put it.[53]

Outraged, Chinese living in Paris held a stormy meeting and then blockaded their country's delegation in its hotel to prevent them going to Versailles for the signing ceremony. Balfour charged China with ingratitude since, 'without the expenditure of a single shilling or the loss of a single life' it had been 'restored to her rights which she could never have recovered for herself'. But, Japan's record left others in the British delegation, not to mention Wilson, sceptical. Curzon pressed Japan to name a date on which they would hand back the peninsula and lined up with the Americans to try to get Tokyo to soften its policy towards China. To no avail. No date was set.[54]

In Peking, students angered by news of the agreement in Versailles attacked the homes of pro-Japanese politicians in protests that mutated into the May Fourth Movement which, with its call for the country to have a 'Mr Science' and a 'Mr Democracy', became the fulcrum for calls for modernisation and democracy, influencing a wide sweep of intellectuals and writers, including Mao Tse-tung. Though the May Fourth Movement's practical impact was limited by the warlord era and the subsequent 'Confucian Fascism' of Chiang Kai-shek's Nationalist regime established in 1927, it remains one of the leitmotifs of twentieth century China and for hopes of rational dialogue rather than habitual use of force to settle arguments.[55]

Delegates from southern China to a conference designed to seek national unity demanded that Peking denounce all wartime agreements with Japan and refuse the loss of Shantung. This was rejected by northern warlords who preferred to seek accommodation with Tokyo. The conference collapsed and eight years of national anarchy ensued.

Anti-Japanese boycotts were staged at regular intervals and there were mass protests in Shantung and other regions. Japan did not react. Unlike 1895, when it had ceded part of its gains from China under pressure from Western powers, it now had the agreement of Britain, France, Italy and Russia plus the confidence of two victories over European armies and navies – and a contempt for what it called China's 'five minute patriotism'.[56]

A Poisoned Heritage

The relationship between the two main powers of East Asia was at the same time complex and simple. The complexities reach back into the era when China ruled supreme and stretch through to the haven Japan provided in the late imperial era for revolutionaries including the 'Father of the Republic' Sun Yat-sen. In the first half of the twentieth century, matters were simpler as expansionists in Tokyo saw Manchuria and Mongolia, and then the rest of China as lands to be exploited and colonised – and used as a base for the eventual showdown with the Soviet Union for territorial and ideological supremacy. Though the Shantung concessions were formally returned to China in 1922, Japan maintained a military presence there, ostensibly simply to defend its residents in the province, plus effective control of the railway. Divided by the internal struggles of the warlord decade, China was in no position to do anything about this.

Even after the Nationalists formed their government in Nanjing in 1927 under Chiang Kai-shek, China remained weak. In the spring of 1928, Japanese soldiers clashed with Chinese troops in the capital of Tsinanfu. It was not clear who started the trouble but the Japanese stormed a government building, killing sixteen of the staff and, by one report, cutting out the tongue of an official before shooting him in the head. Japanese guns pounded the old city and Chinese soldiers were ambushed as they marched out. Hallett Abend of *The New York Times* put the death toll at 6000. Anti-Japanese demonstrations and boycotts were staged in Shanghai, Canton and Wuhan but Chiang, who was involved in a major struggle with northern militarists, advised his fellow citizens to hide their feelings, building up their thirst for revenge until they could fight back.

That was a long way off as Japan continued its expansion. Finding the ex-bandit warlord who ruled Manchuria insufficiently pliant, hawkish Japanese officers in the Kwantung concession based in the regional capital of Mukden assassinated him by blowing up his train. They thought that his morphine-addicted son, Zhang Xueliang, would be more amenable but he allied with Chiang and resisted pressure. So, in September 1931, while Zhang was away in Peking, the Japanese staged an incident which they blamed on the Chinese and used to take over the whole of the northeast. From there, they expanded steadily into northern China before full-scale warfare broke out between Japan and China after a minor clash at the Marco Polo Bridge outside Peking in early July 1937, which marked the start of the Second World War in East Asia.

That conflict cost anywhere from 14 to 20 million lives, many of them Chinese civilians caught in the fighting. It devastated much of China, notably the more advanced regions of the country. Floods of refugees were uprooted, Japan's rule was brutal and did nothing to convince the Chinese of the 'civilising' mission Tokyo promulgated. Its troops were guilty of recurrent atrocities, most notably the Rape of Nanking. Tokyo tried to set up a collaborationist regime headed by one of Chiang's former colleagues and rivals, but it was a tragic pantomime.

The Nationalist forces, in uneasy alliance with the Communists, were driven back to their refuge in Chongqing behind the Yangtze Gorges, fighting more battles than is generally recognised but, basically, waiting for the United States to defeat Japan. By the time of that victory in 1945, China was exhausted and the Nationalist regime largely discredited among its own people. Four years on, the Communist marched to power; Mao told a Japanese delegation which came to apologise for their country's behaviour that, without Japan's invasion, the movement he led would never have won the civil war.

As it concentrated on economic development from the late 1970s and welcomed Japanese investment, the Chinese authorities forgot the past. But the 1990s saw the launch of a 'patriotic education' programme which told of the 'century of humiliation' at the hands of foreign powers, Japan prominent among them. China's anger at the past was helped by the halting apologies from across the sea. In the second decade of the twenty-first century, confrontation welled up over a group of rocky, uninhabited islands off Japan's southern coast which China also claimed. Tokyo, which had previously been content to kowtow to Beijing, reacted more assertively under its new Prime Minister Shinzo Abe. The new Chinese leader, Xi Jinping, made national strength and military prowess a centrepiece of his 'China Dream'.

The two countries were back on an old track dating back to the end of the nineteenth century. The clash in Tsingtao in 1914 forms part of a saga with a present-day resonance. Given the region's economic and strategic importance, the relationship between China and Japan is important not only for the two nations involved, but for Asia as a whole and for the whole world. The siege that took place under the rain on the Shantung peninsula a hundred years ago thus retains its relevance for our time.

NOTES

WO. FO – War Office, Foreign Office files at Public Records Office, London

NCH – *North China Herald*. Weekly compilation of the *North China Daily News of Shanghai*

NYT – *The New York Times*

FER – *Far Eastern Review*

1   *Watchman*, Diary of Jakob Neumaier quoted in Burdick, p. 71.

2   WO106/662.

3   Note, Asquith papers box 111, quoted in Nish, p.140.

4   Lone gives an excellent account of the war as a whole which is summarized in Fenby, China, pp 49-50; Port Arthur, see Allan. pp. 66-7, 79-91; Creelman, Chapter 5 and his despatches in the New York World Dec 17-19 gives a controversial account of Japanese conduct and is described in Dorwart, pp. 106-11; Eastlake and Yoshi-aki give an admiring contemporary account of Japanese prowess.

5 Kaiser, Massie, p. 180.

6 Attacks, Bottle, Fenby, China, pp. 81-2.

7 Kaiser, Massie, p. 180.

8 Bishop, Massie, p. 33.

9 Schreker gives a comprehensive account of the acquisition of the concession on pp. 29-30 and its subsequent history, Heyking, p. 31.

10 Tsingtao, Forsyth, pp. 113-128.

11 Forsyth, p. 283, description, pp. 113-128.

12 Meyer-Waldeck, Burdick, p. 18; Eberhard von Mantey in: Deutsches Biographisches Jahrbuch, Bd.X: Das Jahr 1928, Stuttgart 1931, s. 172-176.

13 http://query.nytimes.com/gst/abstract.html?res=F7 091FF73A5412738DDDA00894DB405B838CF 1D3; coal, Jones, pp. 166-7.

14 Limitations on German influence, Second, Schrecker, Ch 5, pp. 8-11; Visitors, Jones, p. 169.

15 Treaties, Duus, pp. 277-8.

16 Visit, Massie, pp. 182-3.

17 Forces, balloons, aircraft, Meyer-Waldeck statement after siege, Jones pp. 102-3; Burdick, pp. 19, 48.

18 Emden, Triumph, Corbett, pp. 142-5, 147, 156; Shells, British, French, Burdick, pp. 49, 59; Governor, Jones, p. 28.

19 Diary, WO106/662.

20 Report, WO106/660.

21 Burdick, note 58, pp. 223-4.

22 Japanese statements, Germans, Jones, pp. 34-6.

23 Hand back, Washington, Schrecker, p. 246.

24 Grey, FO37/017, Burdick, note 56, p. 223.

25 Council, Jones, pp. 10-14.

26 Landing, advance, WO106/666.

27 Kuhlo word, Burdick, p. 62.

28 WO Diary, W0106/662; Kaiser, Edgerton, Robert, Warriors of the Rising Sun (New York: Basic Books, 1999), p. 227.

29 Diary, WO106/662.

30 Barnardiston, WO106/665 and London Gazette, May 30, 1916.

31 NCH, Oct 31, 1914.

32 Report WO106/666.

33 Singing, Burdick, p. 142.

34 FO371/2381, Nish, p. 132.

35 NCH, Oct 31, 1914.

36 NCH, Oct 31, 1914.

37 Burdick, pp. 122-3.

38 Grave, Addressed, Burdick, p. 126.

39 Inn, bridges, Jones, p. 57.

40 Cavalry, shells, ceasefire, corpses, Jones, pp. 58-9.

41 Jones, pp. 71-4.

42 NCH, Nov 14.

43 Barnardiston, London Gazette, May 30, 1916; You made me love you, prisoners, NCH, Oct 31, 1914.

44 Kaiser, Burdick, p. 154.

45 NCH, Nov 28, 1914; Leaflets, chaos, Burdick, pp. 74, 166.

46 Representative, Emperor, Burdick, pp. 190-22.

47 History, Corbett, p. 385.

48 Americans, British, Macmillan, pp. 339-40.

49 Alliance, Nish, pp. 156, 193; Macmillan, p. 339.

50 Curzon, Macmillan, p. 339.

51 Wilson, Macmillan, p. 347.

52 Wilson, Macmillan, p. 347, Nicolson, pp. 146-7.

53 Review, NYT, July 27, 1919.

54 Balfour, Nish, p. 274.

55 Rana Mitter's *Savage Revolution* (Oxford University Press, 2004) gives a comprehensive account of the movement.

56 Patriotism, FER, NYT, July 27, 1919.

BIBLIOGRAPHY

Allan, James, *Under the Dragon Flag* (London. Heinemann, 1898)

Burdick, Charles B., *The Japanese Siege of Tsingtau* (Hamden, Conn: Archon Books, 1976)

Corbett, Sir Julian S., *Official History of the Great War: Naval Operations, Vol. I* (London: Longmans, Green and Co. 1920)

Creelman, James, *On the Great Highway* (New York: Lothrop, 1901)

Dorwart, Jeffery M., *The pigtail War* (Amherst: University of Massachusetts Press, 1975)

Duus, peter, ed. *The Cambridge History of Japan* (Cambridge University Press, 1988)

Eastlake, F. Warrington and Yoshi-Aki, Yamada, *Heroic Japan: A History of the war between China & Japan* (Yokohama: Kelly and Walsh, ltd (no date))

Forsyth, Robert Coventry, ed., Shantung, *The Sacred Province of China* (Shanghai: Christian Literature Society, 1912)

Jones, Jefferson, *The Fall of Tsingtau* (Wilmington: Scholarly resources, Inc., 1973)

Lone, Stewart, *Japan's First Modern War* (London: St Martin's Press, 1994)

Macmillan, Margaret, *The Peacemakers* (London: John Murray, new edition 2003)

Massie, Robert K., *Castles of Steel* (London: Jonathan Cape, 2004)

Mitter, Rana, *Bitter Revolution* (Oxford: OUP, 2005)

Mitter, Rana, *China's War with Japan 1937-1945: The Struggle for Survival* (London: Penguin Books, 2013)

Nicolson, Harold, *Peacemaking, 1919* (London: Constable & Co Ltd, 1933)

Nish, Ian H., *Alliance in decline: A Study in Anglo-Japanese Relations 1908-23* (University of London: The Athlone Press, 1972)

Schrecker, John E., *Imperialism and Chinese Nationalism: Germany in Shantung* (Cambridge, Mass: Harvard University Press, 1972)

FURTHER READING AND
ACKNOWLEDGEMENTS

Charles Burdick's *The Japanese Siege of Tsingtau* (Hamden, Conn, Archon Books, 1976) is the fullest account of the events in English and contains much material sourced from German archives in particular on which I drew for this book. Jefferson Jones's *The Fall of Tsingtau* (Boston; Houghton Mifflin, 1915 and Wilmington: Scholarly resources 1973) contains eyewitness material from the Allied side.

Stewart Lone in *Japan's First Modern War* (London; Macmillan, 1994) lays out the 1894–95 conflict with both clarity and detail. Ian Nish's *Alliance in Decline* (London; Athlone, 1972) gives an excellent account of Anglo-Japanese relations 1908–23 that provides context for the Tsingtao story as do the relevant sections of Volume Six of *The Cambridge History of Japan* edited by Peter Duus (Cambridge1988). Nish's *The Origins of the Russo-Japanese War* (London; Longman, 1985) does a similar job for that conflict.

Two books by Rana Mitter provide first-rate accounts of what came after Tsingtao – *Bitter Revolution* (OUP Oxford 2005) charts the May Fourth Movement and

China's War with Japan (London: Allen Lane, 2013) is the best English-language account of the 1937–45 conflict. My own *Penguin History of Modern China* (London; Penguin, second edition 2013) provides the Chinese story of the relationship since the 1894 with particularly emphasis on the Nationalist era, and the general Chinese context.

The Baptist Mission's book on *Shantung, The Sacred Province of China* (Shanghai; Christian Literature Society 1912) gives the best picture of the province and Tsingtao just before the war, though obviously from a Western missionary viewpoint.

Margaret Macmillan's *The Peacemakers* (London: John Murray, new edition 2003) is the outstanding book on the Versailles Peace Conference with its Japanese and Chinese elements.

The North China Herald, published in Shanghai and drawing together the reports of the *North China Daily News*, contains lively front-line reporting of the battle. A complete set can be consulted at the School of Oriental and African Studies (SOAS) in London. British official records are at the Public Records Office at Kew. I am grateful to the staffs of both institutions for their help.